A Practical Guide To Corals

For The Reef Aquarium

Ed Puterbaugh
Eric Borneman

"Be still, and observe in awe the magnificent splendor of the oceans."

— Anonymous

Published by:

Crystal Graphics
2891 Richmond Rd. Suite 102
Lexington, Kentucky 40509
1-606-266-4888

First printing September 1996
Second printing March 1997
Graphic Design by Chris Reding and Sean Sears of Crystal Graphics

Acknowledgments and Credits

Many thanks to the hundreds of dealers, distributors, and hobbyists who have helped in this project. In particular, we would like to thank the following people for their special level of help and support:

Charles Delbeek, Frank Greco, John Tullock, Kevin Gaines, Morgan Lidster, Bruce Davidson, Noel Curry, James Kwee, Robbert Macare', Scott Woerner, Carl DelFavero, Michael Kamai, Byron Rashed, Kevin Fitzpatrick, Darian Odabasi, Bryon Caenepeel, Butch Almberg, Steve Rader, Terry Fields, Eric Cohen, Scott Cohen, Bob Stern, Bryan Jones, David Lorbiecki, Marlee McDonald, Rich and Rose Heite, Ron and Peggy German, Albert Theil, Hugo and Eleanor Borneman, Jan Burke, Nancy Bronner, Erin Puterbaugh and Aaron Shelley, and J.R.

A special thanks to J.E.N. (Charlie) Veron for reviewing the book and providing invaluable input for the second printing.

Our apologies to anyone we accidentally omitted.

Library of Congress Cataloging-in-Publication Number 96-86765

ISBN# 0-945738-99-4

DEDICATION

This book is dedicated to the nicest person I know, my wife Nancy.

In April of 1995, my family and I were in a horrible one car accident on a winding mountain road in rural Tennessee. My daughter Erin had to wear a brace for several months. My wife Nancy had to have spinal surgery twice in three weeks, and was facing many months of rehabilitation. During a long period of depression for Nancy, I installed a 75 gallon reef tank to help take her mind off her pain and misery. It was one of the most therapeutic things I could have possibly done. A reef tank is an incredibly dynamic environment, always something new to see. Even our battle with the Mantis shrimp was a real adventure for someone flat on their back.

As we started stocking our tank, I told Nancy about all of the wonderful things available in our local pet stores. "Show me" she would say, so I bought every book about corals that I could find. Wilkens, Veron, Humann, Sprung and Delbeek all became familiar names in our house. While we learned a tremendous amount from all of these books, I still could not show Nancy half of the things that the dealers had to offer. We couldn't believe that someone had not published a "practical" guide for the hobbyist. The more I researched things, the more I knew that a book like this was way overdue. They say that necessity is the mother of invention, so the idea for a book was born. Of course owning a graphic design and printing company doesn't hurt.

HOW THIS BOOK WAS WRITTEN

As I posted a lot of inquiries on-line, it became apparent that the majority of hobbyists, dealers and distributors were almost as befuddled as Nancy and I. Frank Greco, the Director of the Fish and Marine Life division of America On-line and Head Aquarist of the Aquarium for Wildlife Conservation in Brooklyn, was instrumental in helping me draft a preliminary species list organized by scientific names. Eric Borneman, Pet Host for the Fish and Marine Life division, became co-author on the project. Of course the list grew and evolved over the next several weeks as I communicated with hundreds of dealers and hobbyists.

When the list was compiled, I sent it out to over 300 dealers all over the country. I wanted a basic response to all of the scientific names on the list — "What do YOU call this?". Almost every dealer responded to the survey. Some knew every scientific name on the list, but as a rule, most knew only a few. From these responses, we picked what we felt were the most prevalent and descriptive common names for each species while avoiding the duplicity of names that has plagued the hobby. After the book was designed, we once again sent out hundreds of "beta" copies to dealers. We took this unusual approach of allowing widespread review before publication because we wanted this to be a useful tool for hobbyists everywhere.

We know that there are some things in this book that are going to be controversial. We welcome criticism because we feel that dialog is essential to growth and understanding. For those who choose to disagree with our "practical" approach, it is important to keep in mind that the specimens and nomenclature are not just a product of what Eric and I thought should be in the book. It is the collective works of those 300 dealers who responded to our surveys. This project has truly been a labor of love for the beautiful creatures in our reef tanks. I hope that reef keepers everywhere benefit from our efforts.

By the way, Nancy is now walking over 5 miles every morning and recovering nicely.

Ed Puterbaugh

About The Authors

Ed Puterbaugh

Ed is an accomplished photographer, author and publisher with a life long love of animals and the environment. He is an avid whitewater and sea kayaker, hiker, camper, and trout fisherman. He received a B.A. in Microbiology from the University of Kentucky and worked as a clinical microbiologist diagnosing bacterial diseases for several years. However, he found that he preferred a less structured lifestyle to the sterile environment of a clinical laboratory. After building a passive solar home for himself and his wife, Ed went on to build 52 hybrid solar homes in the Lexington area, a record for the state of Kentucky. He currently owns Crystal Graphics, a graphic design and publishing company in Lexington.

Ed fell in love with the coral reef environment while snorkeling on the reefs of the Florida Keys, Hawaii, the Bahamas and especially Belize. He is a strong supporter of reef conservation, humane collection techniques (fish and corals) and aquaculture. He believes that coral reef keeping as a hobby is helping to develop husbandry and propagation techniques that will ultimately help save our fragile coral resources from extinction in the wild.

Ed can be reached through e-mail at Octocoral@aol.com.

Eric Borneman

Known as "Eric Hugo" to many on-line hobbyists, Eric was born in 1965 in Pasadena, California. He received a B.A. from Rice University in 1987, with an emphasis in vertebrate biology. Having snorkeled reefs since the age of seven, he became a certified diver at the age of 12 and has maintained a fascination with coral reefs since that time. His main interest in the hobby has been in attempts to create natural and healthy microcosms that resemble the reef itself. He is actively promoting reef conservation through the hobby, and assisting others to keep more successful reef aquaria.

He is currently a Pet Host for the Fish and Marine Life division of America On-line, specializing in reefs. He is also a help staff member of the Aqualink web site for marine aquaria. He has written numerous articles for Marine Fish Monthly and various sites throughout the internet. While there are many exciting reef related projects "in the works", he is currently authoring several other books and articles. He has been keeping his beloved reef aquariums for over seven years, and loves them as much as the day he began.

Eric can be reached through e-mail at Erichugo@aol.com.

The Photography

The photography in this book was accomplished through the use of a high quality 35mm digital camera using no film or chemical processing. All of the photographs are originals taken in dealer and hobbyist tanks all over the country using only natural lighting. We made a conscious decision to present specimens just the way you would find them in local pet stores. This presented a few quandaries that you should be aware of as you read this book.

The specimens that we photographed were typically small and may change shape and color as they grow. We recommend that you review some of the other books that we mention in the index. This will give you a better idea of what many of the corals will look like when they mature.

Many of the aquariums and specimens had problems and imperfections. While we could have easily found picture perfect replacements, we have tried to take the opportunity to point out these problems throughout the book. With this knowledge, a perceptive hobbyist will be able to make better decisions about buying healthy specimens.

Table of Contents

IMPORTANT NOTE!

For many years, there has been a ban on the collection of all stony corals from the waters of Florida, the Gulf of Mexico, and the Caribbean Sea. The ban does not include soft corals and gorgonians that are regularly offered from this region. This ban was placed into effect to prevent the degradation of an already small reef system that did not have the natural reserves that exist in the vast reef areas of the Indo-Pacific. However, in recent years there has been much progress in the field of aquaculture and captive propagation techniques which may allow for more species of this region to become widely available. These captive breeding and propagation facilities, if maintained in the interests of the captive bred species, should be supported not only for the quality and adaptability of the organisms to a closed system, but also to minimize any further degradation to the natural reefs through improper collection practices.

Introduction

Only in recent history has the advent of scuba and marine aquariums brought the realm of the underwater world into the lives and reach of everyone. Consequently, the reef environment has not had much time to develop proper taxonomic classifications. Most people initially thought corals were either rocks or plants, so naturally identifying and naming all the "pretty fish" came first. Thus, the discovery of the vast array of coral species has been comparatively recent, and it is still far from complete. Standardization has been far more prevalent with marine fish than with corals and invertebrates. At least everyone agrees that a yellow tang is a yellow tang. Yet, several completely different species of corals have been commonly referred to as "Meat"! To say the least, there have been many confusing inconsistencies in the nomenclature that often resulted in the improper identification of coral species.

There is still so much to be learned about the corals of the reefs. For example, the astounding array of color morphs within a species makes it very hard to call an apple and apple, so to speak. How can there be a universally recognized "red mushroom," when there are probably four hundred different shades of red mushrooms, some with stripes, some with bumps, and all from different parts of the world? Does it make sense to use skeletal cues to scientifically classify animals that by definition have no true skeleton?

We have spent countless hours assimilating established taxonomy, studying reference material, and sorting surveys concerning the name most commonly used for a species. In some cases, there was no common name for a coral, for others there were several. We have attempted to associate the most universally recognized common name with a species, except where two corals shared the same common name. When a choice was necessary, we attempted to pick the one that most closely approximated the appearance or character of the coral.

Born out of frustration, this book attempts to forever end the experience of requesting a Brain coral and receiving a Flowerpot. The reader should no longer wonder why there are three different Plate corals in a local store that are obviously entirely different animals. We hope that there will, at last, be some standardization of common nomenclature between collectors, shippers, CITES inspectors, wholesalers, retailers, hobbyists, and the inquisitive house guest who will invariably ask, WOW, what is that?. It will be a gradual process to begin calling a five year old coral by a new name. Now retail stores will no longer have an excuse to simply write "Meat" coral on the front of their display tank.

"What is that?" asks the child standing in front of the gorilla cage.

"It's a monkey," replies the unknowing parent.

Well perhaps, but this is not an accurate portrayal or identification.

This book is hopefully a light that will grow over time to dispel the darkness that surrounds such a problem. This is a type of ignorance that needs to be avoided...

not only for the sake of proper classification,

not only for the ultimate protection of the fragile reef ecosystem,

but for the benefit of the all who participate in the care of these beautiful, fascinating, and remarkable animals called corals.

Eric and Ed

The Care Charts

Lighting Needs	5 - 9
Water Flow	L - M
Aggressiveness	H
Difficulty of Care	8

There are care charts throughout the book to help reef keepers make informed decisions about proper environmental conditions in their aquariums. While the recommendations given will be true for the majority of specimens, these are only guidelines based on the conditions in which the coral is found in nature, and from the experiences of experts and hobbyists. There will certainly be specimens that fail to thrive in the recommended conditions. Similarly, many people will have corals that thrive in conditions other than the ones suggested. A myriad of variables exist, from the actual place of specimen collection, to specific conditions within a hobbyist's tank, that make the exact care needs of individual corals impossible to ascertain. Even though general recommendations are given in this book, the aquarist should take the time to investigate thoroughly the exact requirements of any coral, and the correct methods of establishing and running reef aquaria. Finally, all reef tanks should be supplemented with a minimum of additions that include calcium, strontium, and iodine.

Lighting:

Hermatypic corals have symbiotic algae contained within their tissues called zooxanthellae. These algae help meet some or all of the energy needs of the coral host through photosynthesis. Consequently, lighting is one of the most important parameters for the success of hermatypic corals in the reef aquarium. It is also, to a large degree, responsible for the myriad of colors with which corals are endowed. A full description of the immense importance that lighting serves in the reef aquarium is beyond the scope of this book.

> **Level 1 — Very little to no direct light.**
>
> **Level 6 — The most intense lighting possible under normal fluorescent lights.**
>
> **Level 8 — The most intense lighting possible using VHO fluorescent or Power Compacts.**
>
> **Level 10 — Direct Metal Halide lighting.**

Water Flow Requirements:

Another variable that is important in the success of corals, and especially in their ability to fully expand, is the amount of water flow to which they are exposed. Some specimen's polyps will not expand fully if there is a constant hard wash of water over them,. Other coral polyps will not extend at all unless the buffeting action of water is suggestive of the wave action found in the reef shallows where they are found. Most of the SPS corals prefer this type of condition.

> **Low — Water that has a constant yet very slow, almost unnoticeable flow.**
>
> **Medium — Lifts and blows polyps, like a breeze blows grass. Noticeable, but not forceful.**
>
> **High — Obviously forceful and whipping action that is like sheets of rain and wind in a storm. It is deliberately strong, but not damaging.**

IMPORTANT NOTE:

The best current in any situation is a random or rhythmic current that allows the natural flex and bend of coral polyps. This allows for the most efficient removal of toxins and waste products from the coral itself.

Aggressiveness:

The aggressiveness of corals is important in determining their placement relative to other species. A strongly aggressive coral can kill nearby corals very rapidly, an unnecessary expense and loss of life. It is important not to overcrowd a reef aquarium, since most corals can be expected to grow, and will eventually infringe on neighboring corals. Coral aggressiveness is determined by the strength of the nematocysts (stinging cells), degree of expansion, presence and length of sweeper tentacles, potential growth rate, and, in the case of soft corals, terpenoid and mucous release. While in nature, aggressiveness is important in the competition for food and space, it is often less than desirable in our aquaria.

Low — Can be placed quite near other species with little concern that it will cause harm (although lit may easily be harmed by others).

Medium — Will harm others placed in immediate proximity to them, but should not be a threat to nearby corals.

High — Has sufficient structures to allow it to rapidly damage or kill other species anywhere nearby.

Difficulty of Care:

The degree to which a coral can be kept successfully in an aquarium is very important to a hobbyist. While every reef keeper should attempt to keep a microcosm that closely resembles a small section of natural reef, some tanks are better suited to keeping one type of coral over another . For example, a 55 gallon tank with normal output fluorescent lights and many fish is better suited to keeping mushroom anemones and leather corals, while a 180 gallon tank with metal halides and few fish is a good environment for keeping the difficult SPS corals. Difficulty of care is determined by the minimum actual conditions that must be met in order for the coral not merely to survive, but to thrive and grow. It is also determined by a coral's tolerance to changes in water chemistry and conditions.

Level 1 — Can be kept successfully by inexperienced hobbyists with minimal hardware and effort.

Level 5 — Should be kept by those with some experience in captive coral care, and whose tanks are well established and stable environments.

Level 10 — Extremely difficult to care for. Should only be kept by the most experienced hobbyists whose tanks have near perfect water conditions that approach those of the reef itself.

IMPORTANT NOTE:

There is no "best" tank, other than a healthy one. It is important for the aquarist to know his limitations of skill, equipment, and level of bio-load in order to achieve a natural and healthy reef aquarium. Trying to keep fragile corals in an unsuitable environment is a senseless and frustrating waste. In nature, one would not expect to find Acropora in a lagoon or Carnation corals on a reef crest. Obviously, the hobbyist should strive to duplicate the conditions in which a coral would be found on a natural reef. Yet, our ability to successfully keep many species is often limited by our present knowledge of their needs in a closed, captive environment.

Brain, Moon & Pineapple Corals

The brain, moon and pineapple corals are technically a part of the large polyped stony corals. Although there are tremendous differences in shape, texture and color, many dealers have historically referred to the entire group simply as brain corals. Because of their common physical characteristics, they have been presented as a separate chapter.

In general, brain corals resemble brains with a meaty, circuitous appearance. Moon corals, while similar in overall appearance to the brains, look like a moon or ball covered with ovoid craters. Brain corals may be either flat or round, and meandering, while the moon and pineapple corals tend to form solely compact, round colonies. Pineapple simply refers to the brown variations of moon coral.

Brain Corals

There are many species of what are commonly called closed brain corals. Most have round massive heads with either worm-like channels or round "craters" that give them a characteristic appearance that resembles a brain. The open brain corals also have these channels, but the skeletal shape is more flattened, and the coral tissue is heavier and more "meaty" in appearance.

In many cases, it may be difficult to ascertain a species identity with any degree of accuracy because of typically small specimen sizes. There is also a certain amount of variability within members of the same species.

Though not necessary, feeding brain corals is possible when their tentacles are extended. Tentacles often appear surrounding the septa or along the channels, and are usually quite short. All brain corals adapt well to captive conditions if given proper care, and are an attractive and hardy group recommended to the hobbyist.

Lighting Needs	4 - 9
Water Flow	L - M
Aggressiveness	L - M
Difficulty of Care	5

Flat Brain

(Brain, Lobo, Open Brain, Root, Tooth)

Flat Brains have channels, but in a flatter, more open configuration from the round heads typical of other brain corals. Its tissue is heavy and "meaty". There are numerous color morphs, but the most common colors are olive green to brown, and occasionally white, gray-white, and red. These corals can expand dramatically in the aquarium, and are fairly easy to care for if a healthy specimen is chosen. Flat Brains prefer lower current levels than other brain corals.

Scientific Name: Lobophyllia hemprichii

Identification Tip

Unlike the Doughnut Corals (page 35) Flat Brains have meandering lobes and multiple oral openings.

Oral opening

Reproduction by Budding

This "baby" coral head was produced by budding from the parent colony. Each new coral must have its own oral opening.

A new coral starting to form.

Grooved Brain

(Grooved Boulder)

Classically brain-like in appearance, these round headed corals can grow to massive sizes in the wild. In the aquarium, they tolerate many light conditions, and can be expected to thrive. For identification, Grooved Brain can be recognized by its less rounded shape, with an edged bottom and a distinctive groove splitting the hemispheres of the coral head. Like most of the brain corals, it is typically a tan or brown color.

Scientific Name: Oulophyllia crispa

Groove dividing the hemispheres.

Dented Brain

(Brain, Closed Brain, Tooth)

Dented Brain is a fairly difficult species to recognize. Most, but not all, species have a dent or groove along the ridge that separates the open channels. However, this attribute is not always visible when the coral is expanded. While the majority of Dented Brains are round or mostly round, others can be quite flat and opened, such as the one pictured below.

Scientific Name: Symphyllia radians

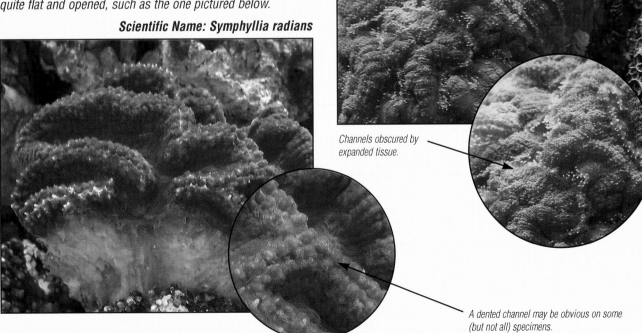

Channels obscured by expanded tissue.

A dented channel may be obvious on some (but not all) specimens.

Swollen Brain

(Red Brain, Red Moon, Swelled Brain)

Swollen Brain species are most noted for their brilliant red morphs, although orange, brown and green are also common colors. Individual polyps can be very large with obvious central mouths. They can obscure the skeleton, making Swollen Brain resemble a colony of mushroom anemones. It prefers slightly lower light and current levels than other brain corals, but is tolerant of other conditions and usually fares well.

Scientific Name: Blastomussa wellsi

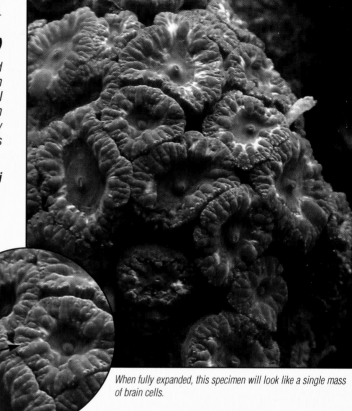

When fully expanded, this specimen will look like a single mass of brain cells.

Individual polyps are a distinguishing feature of Swollen Brain.

Maze

(Brain, Closed Brain, Pineapple)

Maze may be the most recognizable of all brain corals. It has many worm-like channels and is almost exclusively rounded in shape. It can be striking in coloration, with valleys and ridges often contrasted in shades of green, white, and brown. Most species have ridges that are cross-hatched with obvious skeletal teeth, and tissue expansion may be less apparent in these species.

Scientific Name: Platygyra sinensis

Open Brain

Open Brain has the most "open" configuration of all brains. It is typically oval in shape with a single open folded channel. There are two distinct colors of red and green that are commonly available. They are less easy to care for than other brain corals, and iodine is important for their health. Although it may be confused with Flat Brain, Open Brain has a heavy conical base that is typical of substrate dwellers.

Lighting Needs	4 - 8
Water Flow	L - M
Aggressiveness	L
Difficulty of Care	6

Green Open Brain

(Crater, Folded, Puffed)

This green specimen has a slightly more folded appearance than is normally seen.

Scientific Name: Trachyphyllia geoffroyi

Note the typical single folded channel.

Identification Tip

The conical base and figure-eight shape are usually characteristic of Open Brains. However, there is a morphological variation with a a heavy square sided base that has recently started showing up in the hobby. This specimen known as Pacific Rose is often mistakenly imported as Wellsophyllia species. See also Pacific Rose on page 41.

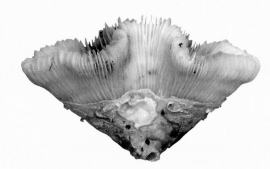

Red Open Brain

(Crater, Folded, Puffed)

Primarily a difference of color only, the red morph does tend to require less light than the green.

Scientific Name: Trachyphyllia geoffroyi

Moon Corals

The moon and pineapple corals, while similar in gross appearance, are a somewhat unclassified and diverse group of species. Moon generally refers to species in which the craters and/or ridges are green or (rare) fluorescent white. Pineapple refers to species in which the craters and ridges are a uniform brown color. Even so defined, there are many striking color variances within these species.

Despite the ambiguity in the actual names of these corals, it seems as though moon and pineapple corals from the genus, Favia, have rounded or oval craters, while those from Favites have craters with usually hexagonal or pentagonal sides arranged in a honeycomb pattern.

Lighting Needs	4 - 9
Water Flow	M
Aggressiveness	L - M
Difficulty of Care	4

Note the shared wall of the corallites.

Brown Moon

Brown Moon is characterized by green craters surrounded by brown ridges.

Scientific Name: Favites abdita

Green Moonstone

Green Moonstone is characterized by an all (or nearly all) green appearance. This coral is very striking, as it is strongly fluorescent under actinic lighting.

Scientific Name: Favia speciosa

Identification Tip

Favia has distinct individual polyps while Favites has a shared wall.

Boulder

(Brain, Star)

Boulder is often called brain coral because of its round appearance, even though it more closely resembles a Pineapple. Though infrequently referred to as such, it is actually most correctly considered a star coral. In nature, this species is rounded in shallow waters and plate-like in deeper waters. Its corallites are elevated from the skeleton and surrounded by obvious toothy ridges. It can be slightly more difficult to care for in the aquarium than other brain corals.

Scientific Name: Montastrea magnistellata

Boulder has pronounced skeletal teeth.

Identification Tip

Because of the general shape and color, specimens such as this one are often incorrectly sold as Moon or Favia. However, the pronounced skeletal teeth are the clue that this is actually a Boulder coral.

Scientific Name: Montastrea curta

Pineapple

Pineapple is characterized by an all (or nearly all) brown coloration, though it resembles Moon in all other aspects.

Scientific Name: Favites flexuosa

Some reports say that brown morphs may be more difficult to keep.

Note the distinct individual polyps characteristic of Favia.

Favia can be blindingly fluorescent under actinic lighting.

Moonstone

Many experts cannot agree on distinctions between species, so it is best to identify these corals through detailed physical descriptions of the color variations. However, Moonstone is suggested as a common name for members of the Favia genus.

Scientific Name: Favia sp.

Large Polyped Stony Corals

The stony corals consist of large and small polyped (SPS) varieties. Although this chapter is concerned with only the large polyped varieties, there is some disservice in the nomenclature, since the size of polyps is a subjective measurement.

Large polyped stony corals, like SPS corals, have a hard skeleton composed of successive layers of calcium carbonate laid down by the polyps. Hence, they need a high calcium level to thrive. Strontium, iodine and other trace elements are necessary for their growth and success.

Stony corals are characterized by easily visible polyps that can expand quite dramatically in some species. While requiring excellent water parameters, most are somewhat tolerant of lighting and nutrient levels. The stony corals still require fairly strong illumination, but most can be kept under sufficient fluorescent lighting. Preference for water flow depends on the species.

They generally reproduce either by spawning or by "budding," a process where a small version of the parent grows and separates, forming a new colony. Reproduction of stony corals in a well run reef tank is fairly common.

Feeding most stony corals is not necessary, although many will accept small pieces of food, such as bits of shellfish, crustaceans, squid, and even fish. Other ahermatypic (or zooxanthellae lacking) corals require feedings for their survival.

One feature common to many species is the presence of surprisingly long "sweeper tentacles". These elongated tentacles are designed to sting and kill neighboring corals, so care must be used when placing corals with these structures too close to other species.

Anchor

(Hammer, Hammerhead, Sausage, Wall)

Anchor is a commonly available species that is regularly available in green, brown or greenish-pink colors. Like most Euphyllia species, it can send out long and powerful sweeper tentacles, so it must be placed a safe distance away from neighboring corals and invertebrates. This coral is recognized by long graceful polyps that sway beautifully in the current.

Scientific Name: *Euphyllia ancora*

Identification Tip

Anchor has very distinct curved or kidney shaped polyp tips, while those of Hammer are T-shaped. This is a distinction that has not generally been recognized and many species may be misidentified.

Are these two different species, or is this simply a physical morph? We will leave that up to the taxonomists to sort out. It is important for the collector to realize that these two variations occur on a very regular basis. To further complicate the situation, there are also branching varieties of both types, as shown on the following page.

Lighting Needs	4 - 9
Water Flow	L - M
Aggressiveness	H
Difficulty of Care	5

Hammer

(Anchor, Hammerhead, Sausage, Wall)

Hammer is similar in all aspects to Anchor, except that the polyp extremities have more T-shaped ends resembling a hammer. Both Hammer and Anchor, though light tolerant, may have a very specific location in the tank that allows for maximum expansion and health.

Scientific Name: *Euphyllia sp.*
(See Identification Tip above)

Hammer has T-shaped ends that resemble a hammer.

Branching Hammer

Scientific Name: Euphyllia parancora

Following the taxonomical nomenclature of E. parancora to the right, and E. paradivisa (not shown), should this species be called E. parafimbriata?

Branching Anchor

Scientific Name: Euphyllia parancora

Both these species have a skeleton separated by branches. The emerging polyps, like their non-branching relatives, have either anchor or hammer shaped tips.

Lighting Needs	4 - 9
Water Flow	L - M
Aggressiveness	H
Difficulty of Care	5

Frogspawn

(Fine Grape, Flower Pot, Grape, Octopus, Vase, Wall, Zig-Zag)

Frogspawn is recognized by masses of rounded tips that resemble the egg mass of a frog. It is typically found in white, green, pink, or brown shades. Care is similar to other Euphyllia species.

Scientific Name: Euphyllia divisa

Branching round polyp tips look like a mass of "spawn".

Lighting Needs	4 - 9
Water Flow	L - M
Aggressiveness	H
Difficulty of Care	5

Torch

(Branch, Branching Hammer, Green Torch, Pom-Pom)

Torch has a branching skeleton with single tipped polyps. When the polyps are extended, each branch resembles a torch. This specimen is unusual because it has both green and brown variations within the same colony.

Scientific Name: Euphyllia glabrescens

Single tipped polyps.

Grape

(Anchor, Fine Grape, Hammer, Sausage)

Grape coral is the most difficult Euphyllia species to keep, but it is by no means impossible. It too has a branching skeleton, but the polyps extend out with enough mass to obscure the base. The ends of the tentacles have small spheres like Frogspawn.

Scientific Name: *Euphyllia paradivisa*

Lighting Needs	4 - 9
Water Flow	L - M
Aggressiveness	H
Difficulty of Care	6

Note the branching nature of the colony.

Mass of round polyps.

White Grape

Scientific Name: *Euphyllia yaeyamaensis*

An unusual white morph from a very established tank

Identification of Euphyllia Species

Common Name	Base	Polyps
Anchor	Solid	Anchor shaped tips
Branching Anchor	Branching	Anchor shaped tips
Hammer	Solid	T-shaped tips
Branching Hammer	Branching	T-shaped tips
Frogspawn	Solid, Massive	Mass of round tips
Grape	Branching	Mass of round tips
Torch	Branching	Single tips

Bubble Corals

Bubble corals are a spectacular group that can inflate balloon-like vesicles to an amazing size. Oddly enough, these bubbles are not polyps, but are modified tentacles that protect the delicate polyps below them. Caution must be used to avoid tearing the delicate expanded vesicles. These corals can send out short sweeper tentacles that are very powerful. All Bubble corals prefer bright light and low to medium current so the bubbles can inflate maximally. They are tolerant of other conditions.

Lighting Needs	3 - 9
Water Flow	L - M
Aggressiveness	H
Difficulty of Care	4

Short, but powerful sweeper tentacle.

Bubbles normally obscure the mouth of this dramatically expanded specimen.

Bubble

(Bladder)

This common species has large, elongated, white or cream colored bubbles with fine lines on their surface.

Scientific Name: Plerogyra sinuosa

Octobubble

(Bladder, Bubble, Pearl)

Octobubble is very similar to Bubble, except that the vesicles have pimple-like protrusions on them. The bubbles also tend to be slightly smaller.

Scientific Name: Plerogyra sp. (possibly P. symplex)

Note the elongated pimples that may resemble the tentacles of of an octopus, however remotely.

Pearl

(Bubble, Small Bubble, Octobubble, Pearl Bubble)

Pearl is closely related to Bubble and Octobubble. However, this species forms larger colonies with numerous smaller, more rounded bubbles.

Scientific Name: Physogyra lichtensteini

Densely clustered round bubbles.

Galaxy

(Brittle, Durian, Green Star, Moon, Scalpel, Star, Tooth)

Galaxy is a fragile and large colony-type coral that is well known for its long and powerful sweeper tentacles. Shipping is often a problem for this coral, and it is rare to have a specimen that is healthy enough to survive in the aquarium. They are typically brown or green colored.

Scientific Name: Galaxea fascicularis

These sweeper tentacles can be deadly to anything nearby.

Lighting Needs	5 - 9
Water Flow	L - M
Aggressiveness	H
Difficulty of Care	8

Crystal

(Galaxy, Moon, Star, Tooth)

The sparkling polyp tips are why this coral is often called Crystal or Star. An entire colony can look like a "galaxy" of stars. This white specimen is an uncommon variety, brown or green being more typical of the species. Its care needs are the same as required for Galaxy.

Scientific Name: Galaxea astreata

The sparkling polyp tips are very distinct.

Fluted Galaxy

At first glance, this coral looks like a brown Crystal. However, the skeleton consists of many exceptionally long fluted corallites, as shown in the inset below. This specimen is a new import and has just started becoming available to reef hobbyists.

Scientific Name: Galaxea sp.

Lighting Needs	5 - 9
Water Flow	L
Aggressiveness	H
Difficulty of Care	8

Starlet

(Star, Lobed Star)

Starlet is a round or pillar shaped coral whose skeleton is marked with star-like eyes. It is very tolerant of temperature and water quality, where it can be found in sediment filled lagoons. It can exist far north of typical tropical reef zones, even to the Carolinas. Solenastrea, and its related genus of Siderastrea, are abundant hardy corals in nature. Unfortunately, they do not show up often in the aquarium trade.

Scientific Name: Solenastrea bournoni

Lighting Needs	2 - 10
Water Flow	L - H
Aggressiveness	M
Difficulty of Care	3

Environmental Note

Despite being an Atlantic species subject to stony coral bans, some species can be found outside of the restricted Caribbean areas. As such, there are coastal areas where this coral can be collected legally. Its hardiness should allow for easy aquaculture in the future.

Disk Corals

Disk is a common aquarium species that is found on soft bottoms in nature. Capable of actually walking around by tissue inflation and deflation, these corals can thrive with bright light and moderate current. They have a unique skeleton composed of many thin radiating teeth.

As a bottom dweller, Disk has a mucous coat containing nematocysts (stinging cells) that aid in feeding. This mucous can seriously injure other corals that it comes into contact with. For this reason, all Disks have a high aggressiveness rating.

Lighting Needs	5 - 9
Water Flow	L - M
Aggressiveness	H
Difficulty of Care	6

Disk

(China Man's Hat, Fungus, Mushroom, Plate, Stubby Plate)

Scientific Name: Fungia sp.

Purple Disk

(China Man's Hat, Purple Fungus, Purple Mushroom, Stubby Purple Plate)

Scientific Name: Fungia danai

Care Tips

As with any flat corals, care should be taken not to trap air bubbles underneath when placing them in the aquarium. Air bubbles cause irritation and may eventually lead to tissue necropsy and death.

Disk corals should never be taken out of the water while inflated. They should be handled very delicately to avoid harming the tissue and protective slime layer.

Long Tentacled Plate

(Plate, Disk, Mushroom, Sunflower)

Long Tentacled Plate is similar in appearance to Disk. It looks more like an anemone because of its thicker, longer, and more numerous tentacles. Like Disk, it appears in several colors, but often has pink tipped tentacles. Care for Long Tentacled Plate is similar to Disk, although it is slightly more fragile.

Scientific Name: Heliofungia actiniformis

Lighting Needs	4 - 7
Water Flow	L - M
Aggressiveness	H
Difficulty of Care	7

This bulging is common upon introduction to new tank conditions.

Helmet

(Dome)

Helmet is related to the other solitary plate-type corals. However, this species is more rounded, resembling an old war bonnet or motorcycle helmet. The tentacles are finer and more numerous than related species, giving it a fuzzy appearance. Its colors can vary, and its care is similar to that of the Disks.

Scientific Name: Halomitra pileus

Lighting Needs	4 - 7
Water Flow	L - M
Aggressiveness	M
Difficulty of Care	7

Elegance Corals

Elegance Corals are very common and successful additions to an aquarium. In nature, their base sits in the substrate with tentacles extending upwards, resembling an anemone. They may act as a surrogate host to clownfish, and can also provide a refuge for other fish. Elegance corals have powerful stinging cells and expand tremendously in the aquarium. In this way, they can injure other corals easily, so care must be taken to give them plenty of space. They enjoy occasional feedings.

Lighting Needs	3 - 8
Water Flow	L - M
Aggressiveness	H
Difficulty of Care	3

Green Elegance

(Comb, Elegans, Elegant, Meat, Wonder)

The most commonly available variety, Green Elegance, is a hardy species with fluorescent green and brown hues often seen with colored tips on its tentacles.

Scientific Name: Catalaphyllia jardinei

Brown Elegance

Brown Elegance does not have the vivid coloration and bright fluorescence of the green variety. This coral is often referred to as Euphyllia picteti, although this is now an incorrect identification.

Scientific Name: Catalaphyllia jardinei

Purple Tipped Elegance

This is an uncommonly available specimen from the Solomon Islands and Jakarta, and is notable for its bright purple-tipped tentacles. Other variations of Elegance include bubble shaped ends and split ends.

Scientific Name: Catalaphyllia jardinei

Candycane

(Candy, Trumpet)

Candycane is an attractive and hardy stony coral. The polyps appear clustered on the end of a stalked skeleton, and are characteristically striped with green accents. They prefer indirect bright light and low current, but can adapt to a wide variety of conditions. The polyps of Candycane are generally more isolated than those of Trumpet, and the tissue remains close to the skeleton.

Scientific Name: Caulastrea furcata

Lighting Needs	3 - 8
Water Flow	L - M
Aggressiveness	L
Difficulty of Care	4

Reduced lighting may cause the striped pattern to disappear.

Both Candycane and Trumpet originate from branching stalks.

Trumpet

(Bullseye, Candy, Candycane)

Trumpet is closely related to Candycane. However, it is usually more clustered, often resembling a ball of coral when expanded. The polyps, though separated on individual stalks, can obscure the branched skeleton and gives it the appearance of a more solid grouping. It is frequently less colorful than Candycane, and prefers higher water movement.

Scientific Name: Caulastrea echinulata

Lighting Needs	3 - 8
Water Flow	M
Aggressiveness	L
Difficulty of Care	4

Identification Tip

The polyps on Trumpet extend further out from the skeleton than on Candycane. When expanded, they look like the horn of a trumpet.

Flowerpot Corals

Flowerpot corals consist of many similar species that are singularly beautiful. They have long, elegant tentacles that sway gracefully in the current, but falsely lure the hobbyist. They are usually found in a green tone with brown or white casts. For identification, the ends of Flowerpot tentacles have twenty four tips. The related Daisy coral (Alveopora) has only twelve.

While there are some people who have apparently kept Flowerpots successfully for years, claiming different methods for success, it is out of the reach of ordinary hobbyists to do so at this time, regardless of claims to the contrary.

Not recommended.

Lighting Needs	4 - 8
Water Flow	L - M
Aggressiveness	M - H
Difficulty of Care	10

Flowerpot

(Ball, Brown Branch, Daisy, False Brain)

This beautiful specimen is typical of a newly introduced Flowerpot with the common ball-like skeleton.

Scientific Name: Goniopora lobata

Branching Flowerpot

(Bouquet, Branching Goniopora)

Branching Flowerpot is a less common branched variation.

Scientific Name: Goniopora eclipsensis ?

Recession typically seen weeks or months after introducing Flowerpot to the aquarium. The course of demise usually starts with polyps that do not extend. Recession begins, and tissue is often rapidly consumed by brown jelly infection.

Fox

(Jasmine, Lettuce, Ridge)

Fox is a beautiful species whose large polyps expand enormously, and then fold over a wavy thin ridge-like skeleton. It prefers dim or indirect light with slow current areas for full expansion. Colors vary in the pale green and light brown shades. Although sometimes described as difficult to keep, most hobbyists have found it to be quite hardy.

Scientific Name: Nemenzophyllia turbida

Lighting Needs	2 - 6
Water Flow	L
Aggressiveness	L
Difficulty of Care	6

Button Corals

Button is a unique single polyp that can inflate to a surprising size in the aquarium. It prefers low current to really inflate, and is tolerant of different light conditions. The tissue is typically translucent and glossy, and it looks easily punctured. Beneath the tissue, thin blade-like teeth are visible. Button can exist in many colors, including shades of brown, white, yellow and green.

Lighting Needs	3 - 6
Water Flow	L
Aggressiveness	L
Difficulty of Care	5

The wet, lacquered look may be a transient phase.

This expanded Button is showing its ring of feeding tentacles.

Button

(Doughnut, Flat Brain, Lacquered Cylinder, Meat Polyp, Phonograph, Tooth)

Scientific Name: Cynarina lacrymalis

Red Button

(Doughnut, Flat Brain, Lacquered Cylinder, Meat Polyp, Phonograph, Tooth)

This Red Button shows a common variation with marbled tissue.

There are obvious physical differences of this specimen from the Buttons of the same species above. This visual discrepancy leads one to question the ambiguities, contradictions, and inadequacies of taxonomic classification that is so prevalent in coral identification.

Scientific Name: Cynarina lacrymalis

Blade-like skeletal teeth help distinguish the Buttons from the Doughnut corals.

Doughnut Corals

Doughnuts are a single polyped species that are often confused with Buttons. Despite their similarity, Doughnuts do not normally puff out as much as Buttons, and rounded skeletal teeth give them a bumpy appearance. They also have a distinct rounded top with a leathery appearance to the tissue. Common color variations are red, brown, or green, and sometimes striped. Doughnuts prefer shaded areas, as they are typically found under ledges in nature.

Lighting Needs	2 - 6
Water Flow	L - M
Aggressiveness	M
Difficulty of Care	6

Multiple oral openings are rare in Doughnuts, but they do occur. However, they are generally found in a single plane instead of in meandering lobes.

Flat Brain with multiple oral openings

Doughnut

(Artichoke, Button, Caribbean Beaker, Flat Brain, Large Cup Mushroom, Meat, Tooth)

Scientific Name: Scolymia australis

Identification Tip

Flat Brains are more meandering than the Doughnut Corals and always have multiple oral openings.

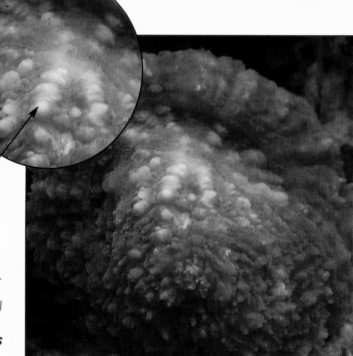

Leathery skin and bumpy skeletal protrusions.

Red Doughnut

Scientific Name: Scolymia vitiensis

Cup Corals

Cup corals are a large group of corals whose species closely resemble each other, despite a large variety of color and shape morphs. While they have characteristically long polyps resembling Flowerpots, their skeleton has raised corallites from which the tentacles emerge. Furthermore, the entire skeleton is covered with skin-like tissue. These corals are demanding of good water conditions, but the precise light and current requirements depend a great deal on the part of the reef from which they were taken.

Lighting Needs	4 - 9
Water Flow	M
Aggressiveness	L
Difficulty of Care	6

Most Cup corals are broken off of larger pieces, but they generally heal well.

Note resemblance of polyps to Goniopora.

Cup

(Bowl, Octopus, Pagoda, Platter, Saucer, Turban, Vase)

Cup corals are usually found in brown and gray tones.

Scientific Name: Turbinaria peltata

Octopus has smaller, more tubular corallites.

Yellow Cup

Yellow Cup, like other Cup corals, often takes the shape of a folded saucer or cup.

Scientific Name: Turbinaria frondens

Octopus

Octopus can be differentiated from Cup by its rubbery looking "skin" and tentacles with short ends that look like the suckers of an octopus.

Scientific Name: Turbinaria patula

Pagoda

(Bowl, Cup, Lettuce, Scroll)

The convoluted shape of Pagoda is simply a morphological variation of either the Cup or Octopus corals. All of the Turbinarians have wide variations in shapes and sizes

Scientific Name: Turbinaria sp. *(possibly T. patula)*

Lighting Needs	4 - 9
Water Flow	M
Aggressiveness	L
Difficulty of Care	6

Yellow Scroll

(Yellow Turbinaria, Yellow Lettuce)

Yellow Scroll is a beautiful yellowish-brown species that can form plates, cups, or convoluted ridges. The skeleton is much thinner and smoother than Pagoda, lacks prominent corallites, and rarely extends tentacles. The flatter specimens are somewhat hardier, requiring less light and water flow.

Scientific Name: Turbinaria reniformis

Lighting Needs	4 - 9
Water Flow	M
Aggressiveness	L
Difficulty of Care	8

Fire Corals

Despite their appearance, Fire corals are not true stony corals, but hydrocorals. They have no polyps, only thin hair like stinging filaments. All Fire corals can cause a painful sting on contact. They are fairly hardy in the aquarium, preferring bright light and strong current.

Common forms include rods, pillars, plates, branches and even encrusting types with a wide array of potential variations. Caribbean species are available only through aquaculture.

Lighting Needs	6 - 10
Water Flow	L - M
Aggressiveness	H
Difficulty of Care	7

Fire corals, as well as other hydrocorals, possess stinging hairs that aid in protection and feeding. Contact with these notorious hairs has been a painful encounter for divers all over the world.

Fire (branching)

(Stinging)

The branching variety of Fire coral has many different species. It is common to both Atlantic and Pacific reefs.

Scientific Name: Millepora alcicornis

Fire (plate)

(Stinging)

This is only one of the several forms of Fire coral.

Scientific Name: Millepora platyphyllia?

Identification Tip

Fire corals are uniformly cream to mustard brown with white edges or tips; a color pattern that is a clear identifier and warning of Fire coral.

LARGE POLYP STONY CORALS

Pipe Organ

(Pipe, Organ Pipe, Red Organ)

Pipe Organ is not a true stony coral, but an octocoral. However, it is included here because it is calcareous. It has a unique skeleton of thin red pipes, with beige or white polyps. Specimens are often broken off from larger colonies, but the fragmented pieces can exist quite well on their own. This coral is prone to attack by bristleworms who eat the polyps and take refuge in the fragile pipes. It is very tolerant of light and current, and is generally easy to keep.

Pipe Organ, like Blue coral, is sold for its dead skeleton, and should never be purchased as a decoration or curio.

Scientific Name: Tubipora musica

Lighting Needs	3 - 10
Water Flow	L - H
Aggressiveness	L
Difficulty of Care	4

Skeleton resembles organ pipes.

Blue Coral

(Ridge)

The only member in its family, Blue Coral is not a true stony coral, either. It is ridge-like or occasionally branching, with a brownish-blue color that is a result of the deposition of iron salts in its calcified skeleton. Because of its white edges, Blue Coral can be mistaken for Fire coral. However, it is not a hydrocoral as it has polyps and does not sting. Dead Blue Coral is regularly sold for its beautiful dried skeleton. Support for this destructive loss of coral can be avoided by refusing to purchase such curios. When alive, Blue Coral will thrive in an aquarium if given strong light and current.

Scientific Name: Heliopora coerulea

Lighting Needs	6 - 10
Water Flow	H
Aggressiveness	L
Difficulty of Care	8

Environmental Note

The skeleton of this coral is only blue when dead and dried. Please do not purchase as a decoration or curio.

Rose Corals

Rose corals look similar to Open Brain and Flat Brain corals. They are a smaller species, usually only a few inches across. Their tissue is not as heavy as Flat Brain and affords a clearer view of the skeleton below. Yet, their skeleton is not conical like the Open Brains. They are commonly found in colors that include pink, brown and blue. Rose corals thrive in conditions similar to those required by brain corals. In fact, the only reason they are not included among them is that they are almost never referred to as such.

Lighting Needs	4 - 8
Water Flow	M
Aggressiveness	M
Difficulty of Care	5

Caribbean Rose

A colored Rose is probably an illegal Caribbean import of the genus Manicina. It is best to inquire about its origin.

Scientific Name: Manicina sp.

Identification Tip

The conical base and figure-eight shape are usually characteristic of Open Brains. However, there is a morphological variation with a a heavy square sided base that has recently started showing up in the hobby. This specimen known as Pacific Rose has been mistakenly imported as Wellsophyllia species.

Pacific Rose

The Pacific Rose is usually a shade of brown and lacks the vibrant colors of its Caribbean counterpart.

Scientific Name: Trachyphyllia geoffroyi

Tissue is not as meaty as Lobophyllia.

When its tentacles are extended, the Pacific Rose will accept small bits of food such as shrimp.

Environmental Alert

A ROSE BY ANY OTHER NAME?

Recently specimens from the Indo-Pacific have been imported as Wellsophyllia species. Because of their comparatively recent appearance and questionable taxonomy, there is a possibility that some specimens are actually black-marketed Caribbean Rose. Every effort should be made to validate the specimen.

Tongue

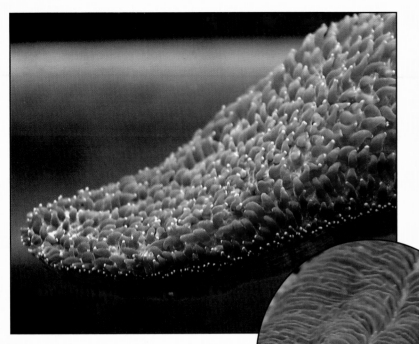

(Sea Mole, Slipper)

Tongue resembles a brown cucumber with fine polyped tentacles covering its surface. It is quite hardy and tolerant of light and current conditions, but prefers to be on a sand or rubble bottom where it may actually move around on the bottom like Disk. The grooved skeleton of Tongue is occasionally branched.

Scientific Name: Herpolitha limax

Lighting Needs	4 - 8
Water Flow	L - M
Aggressiveness	M
Difficulty of Care	5

Identification Tip

Tongue has a prominent groove along the top that distinguishes it from slipper.

Slipper

(Fuzzy Slipper, Hairy Slipper)

Slipper and Tongue are very similar in appearance. The difference between them is that the skeletal body of Slipper does not have grooves on its surface. The polyps also tend to be fuller and thicker on Slipper. They are fairly easy to care for, preferring a sandy bottom and low current with bright light.

Scientific Name: Polyphillia talpina

Lighting Needs	4 - 8
Water Flow	L - M
Aggressiveness	M
Difficulty of Care	6

Some specimens may have branching polyps.

Sun Corals

Sun coral is the name given to a group of zooxanthellae-lacking corals, most commonly available as orange cupped varieties. These corals, along with their black, white and yellow relatives, are easy to care for providing they are out of any direct intense light. In fact, they prefer almost complete cover.

Tubastrea, and related Balanophyllia, require frequent feedings when their tentacles are extended. Newly introduced specimens can be coaxed to feed by blowing brine shrimp juice across the cups from which the tentacles emerge. Contrary to many accounts, feeding a single polyp will not keep the entire colony alive. The entire colony must be fed, as each cup is an individual with its own nutritional requirements. The extra nutrient load into the water must be taken into account before choosing to keep these corals.

Lighting Needs	1 - 3
Water Flow	M
Aggressiveness	L - M
Difficulty of Care	6 - 7

Black Sun

(Black Sun, Black Turret)

Black Sun is a fairly common color variation of its orange relatives. It frequently forms branching colonies.

Scientific Name: Tubastrea micrantha

Sun

(Orange Cup, Orange Turret, Red Polyp, Sunflower, Sun Polyps, Turret)

Scientific Name: Tubastrea faulkneri

The polyps on this Sun coral are just beginning to emerge.

The appearance of a well-fed polyp.

Although far more glorious at night, with proper care and feeding polyps can remain open even during the day.

Whiskers

Whiskers is a very hardy but infrequently encountered coral with a strong resemblance to Elegance. Specimens are usually found in brown, gray, or green tones, though it does not have the striking colors of Elegance. It adapts to almost all aquarium conditions, but prefers low currents that do not overly displace its dramatic tentacles. Like Elegance, it can be fed shrimp and other foods like an anemone.

Scientific Name: *Duncanopsammia axifuga*

Lighting Needs	2 - 9
Water Flow	L - M
Aggressiveness	H
Difficulty of Care	3

Small Polyped Stony Corals

The SPS corals are characterized by very small polyps extending from a conspicuous calcareous skeleton. They are usually branched or plate-like in appearance. On the reef, these corals are found principally in areas of high turbulence and bright light, generally occupying the reef flats. They are easily broken, and frequently reproduce through fragmentation in this way. They can also reproduce through synchronous broadcast spawning that is dependent on the lunar cycle.

SPS corals are generally hard to keep in the aquarium because they require nearly perfect water conditions. They need a stable temperature, and are quite intolerant of fluctuations of even a couple of degrees. They require strong lighting that is generally only afforded by high temperature (Kelvin) metal halide lighting. High strontium (as well as other trace elements) and high calcium levels are very important to their success in a reef aquarium. Yet, SPS corals can grow very rapidly in a healthy tank. They require no feeding and will probably not accept food.

Some species are capable of sending out fairly short but powerful sweeper tentacles, and these corals are thus capable of defending their territory against close neighboring corals. They also compete for space through their rapid growth. Most of the small polyped stony corals appear in varied and often bright colors. However, under strong lighting, the colors may turn more brown as the zooxanthellae adapt to the strong light. In general, species of SPS corals with thick branches are easier to keep than those with thin branches.

The SPS corals are not recommended for inexperienced hobbyists.

Acropora

Acropora is a large genus that consists of over 200 species. Most Acropora are referred to under the general name of Staghorn corals. There are, however, many growth patterns that are not accounted for by this descriptive name. Some other common forms are table, bushy and clustered.

Table has short branches spreading out in a flat table top formation. Bushy has many tightly intertwined branches making a thick bushy mass of branches. Staghorn has sharp antler-like branches forming a more open nest-like colony. Clustered has small colonies of short branches.

These are all very fast growing species if kept in near perfect conditions. Despite their many variations and colors, the actual growth pattern and colors of Acropora may change dramatically in conditions of captive care. Therefore, a species of Acropora sold as purple may well become brown in the aquarium, or vice-versa. Identification of species is often impossible because the small colonies offered for sale may not have taken on the distinct characteristics of a larger mature colony.

Lighting Needs	7 - 10
Water Flow	M - H
Aggressiveness	M
Difficulty of Care	6 - 9

Bluetip

Scientific Name: Acropora loripes

Bushy

Bushy Acropora is so named for its dense and fairly compact growth pattern.

Scientific Name: Acropora aspera

Cats Paw

Cats Paw is a unique Acropora whose branches have fused to make wider members with blunt ends.

Scientific Name: Acropora palifera

Cluster

Cluster Acropora is distinct for its small colonies with short branches and rounded tips.

Scientific Name: Acropora digitifera

Environmental Note

Elkhorn is a very well known Acropora species, but is found only in the tropical Atlantic and the Caribbean and is illegal to collect. It may become available in the near future though aquaculture.

Delicate

Scientific Name: Acropora pulchra

Gem

Gem Acropora has distinct clustered jewel-like tips in various colors.

Scientific Name: Acropora gemmifera

Care Tip

Acropora, and most SPS corals, are capable of releasing digestive strands called acontia filaments. These acontia are aggressive structures used to digest the tissue of adjacent corals, so care must be taken to avoid contact between species.

SMALL POLYP STONY CORALS

Green Acropora

Scientific Name: Acropora valida

Care Tips

Bleaching or color fading is caused by a loss of pigmented zooxanthellae.

Uniform bleaching usually is a sign of a rapid change in temperature or light intensity.

Noble

Scientific Name: Acropora sp.

Pine tree

Scientific Name: Acropora sp.

Broken tips are a common way to reproduce Acropora. This happens naturally through storms and waves in nature. Many Acropora being sold originate from fragmentation.

Purple

Scientific Name:

Bleaching from the base is usually a sign of either inadequate lighting or oxygen toxicity due to improper acclimatization to intense lighting.

Purple Acropora

Scientific Name: *Acropora tenuis*

Paler tips are common in many species, and are a sign of rapid growth.

Bleaching at the tips may be indicative of too much light or unacclimated specimens.

Common Staghorn

There are many species of Acropora that have the classical Staghorn growth formation. Because of difficulty in identifying the small individual specimens, it is often necessary to refer to them by the generic name of Staghorn.

Scientific Name: *Acropora formosa*

Underwater epoxy is a common method of attaching corals to live rock.

Tipped

Acropora cerealis

Brush

Brush Acropora is frequently sold as Table Acropora because of its distinct flat top. However, true Table Acropora colonies are entirely flat with short branches, and their horizontal growth pattern does not allow for the vertical growth and branching that this colony shows.

Scientific Name: *Acropora cytherea*

Table

True Table Acropora is remarkably uniform in maintaining a horizontal growth pattern with very short upward branches. This specimen has been placed in the aquarium at an awkward angle.

Scientific Name: *Acropora sp.*

Yellow

Scientific Name: *Acropora selago*

Although Acopora will grow under VHO lighting, the specimens are generally not as full and robust as those grown under metal halides.

Birds Nest

(Brush, Needle, Pink Nest)

Birds Nest is easily recognized by its thin, sharp, delicate branches. It can grow successfully once it has become established in the tank, but is very sensitive to change and needs gradual light acclimation.

Scientific Name: Seriatopora hystrix

Lighting Needs	8 - 10
Water Flow	M - H
Aggressiveness	M
Difficulty of Care	4 - 10

This specimen has thicker branches than the more typical specimen to the right.

Note easily broken branches. This area can often be overgrown by hair algae, sponsor infection and be an area of recession.

Club Foot

(Cat's Paw, Cluster, Finger, Hard Finger)

Club Foot resembles several other species of branching clustered SPS corals, but can be identified by its normally thicker branches with blunted ends. It is considered a slightly hardier SPS coral in the aquarium. Like other similar species, it appears in many colors with specific requirements dependent on the area from which it was collected.

Scientific Name: Stylophora pistillata

Lighting Needs	7 - 10
Water Flow	M - H
Aggressiveness	M
Difficulty of Care	9

Frilly Cactus

(Leaf, Lettuce)

Frilly Cactus is the most commonly imported species of cactus coral. It grows rapidly and can form a field of leafy plates. All Cactus corals prefer bright light and a brisk current.

Scientific Name: Pavona varians

Lighting Needs	6 - 10
Water Flow	M - H
Aggressiveness	L - M
Difficulty of Care	7

Cactus

(Leaf, Lettuce, Potato Chip)

Cactus is a fairly hardy coral that has a thin ridge-like growth pattern. It is the most light and water tolerant of the small polyped group and will attach to and encrust live rock. The colors are usually mustard to brown.

Scientific Name: Pavona decussata

Identification Tip

The fuzzy, needle-like polyps that extend from the surface identify all species of cactus.

Elephant Nose

Elephant Nose is a unique, bumpy, saucer-like coral. It is indeed very elephantine, from its gray and black color to the protuberances that look like tiny elephant trunks extending from its top surface. The specimen shown is unusually colorful.

Scientific Name: *Mycedium elephantotus*

Lighting Needs	4 - 7
Water Flow	M
Aggressiveness	L
Difficulty of Care	7

Elephant Skin

(Corduroy, Phonograph)

Elephant Skin is a leafy or dish-shaped coral that can form large colonies. It is typically brown or gray with white edges. Elephant skin has distinct raised skeletal ridges randomly scattered across its surface that make it resemble the skin of an elephant. It prefers strong light and current, and is occasionally available as a green morph.

Scientific Name: *Pachyseris rugosa*

Lighting Needs	6 - 9
Water Flow	M - H
Aggressiveness	L
Difficulty of Care	6

Lace Coral

Lace Corals are among the most beautiful corals to be found on wild reefs. However, the small specimens usually available are not nearly as impressive and may be overlooked by unenlightened hobbyists. The robust colonies are fan shaped with stout, but brittle, rounded branches. Lace comes in a variety of colors including cream, red and purple. Cream colored specimens are often confused with Fire Corals and in fact were once included in the Millepora genus. The fragile, easily damaged colonies are generally found on the edges of caves and shaded overhangs. They grow slowly and will do best with moderate, pulsing water flow. Delicate Lace (Stylaster sp.) is similar, but has much finer branching.

Scientific Name: Distichopora sp.

Lighting Needs	1 - 4
Water Flow	L - M
Aggressiveness	L
Difficulty of Care	6

Glowing Ember

The white tips makes this coral look like it is smoldering. This is an uncommonly imported species that is becoming more readily available. It is sometimes found incidentally on Indo-Pacific live rock.

Very little is known about its long term care in reef aquariums, but in nature it is found in caves and overhangs. This is not a true stony coral, but a hydrocoral, closely related to the Fire Corals. Unlike them, however, it grows very slowly and does not have a painful sting.

Scientific Name: Distichopora irregularis

Note: some reviewers have suggested that this may actually be a Bryozoan and not a coral.

Lighting Needs	2 - 4
Water Flow	L
Aggressiveness	L?
Difficulty of Care	?

Horn Corals

Horn Coral can resemble Acropora, but usually has thicker branches, some with grooved ends. Although it is more light tolerant than some other SPS corals, it is still difficult to keep. All species will grow rapidly in the right conditions, and the heavier tissue can soon encrust rock. Horn has very powerful sweeper tentacles that, although comparatively short in length, can be very deadly to neighboring corals. It also has a pronounced ability to exude acontia filaments. Many different colors are available, but a bright fluorescent green is common.

Lighting Needs	7 - 10
Water Flow	M - H
Aggressiveness	H
Difficulty of Care	8

Scientific Name: Hydnophora grandis

Scientific Name: Hydnophora rigida

Hydnophores are raised domes that form where corallites have joined together. This is a distinguishing characteristic of Hydnophora, as well as the source of the genus name.

Horn

(Branch, Knob, Green Velvet Horn)

Scientific Name: Hydnophora exesa

Jewel Corals

Jewel corals are members of the genus, *Porites*. They are so named for the small jewel-like eyes that cover their skeleton. Like velvet corals, jewel corals can take on an astonishing array of colors and growth patterns. Encrusting, boulder-shaped, fingered, club-like, and branching forms are all common. All have very small polyps and prefer to be in areas of high current. While most require intense lighting, there are some species that fare better under slightly subdued light. All jewel corals are non-aggressive and must not be placed near any corals which can harm them.

Lighting Needs	7 - 10
Water Flow	H
Aggressiveness	L
Difficulty of Care	8

Jeweled Toe
(Clubbed Finger)

Jeweled Toe is a branched type with many color variations. It can closely resemble Club Foot and Velvet Finger, but usually has shorter branches and the characteristic eyes on its skeleton. It often forms plates with the "toes" growing upward.

Scientific Name: *Porites antennuata*

Jeweled Finger
(Finger, Jewel Stone)

Jeweled Finger is another common variation of *Porites*. When part of a mature colony, this species has longer branches that take on a noticeably pointed appearance with a strong taper that resembles a finger. It, too, is variable in color. Like the other *Porites* species, Jeweled Finger periodically sheds a waxy coating to regenerate and rid itself of algae and waste from its surface.

Scientific Name: *Porites cylindrica*

Identification Tip

Jewel-like "eyes" are a clear indicator of *Porites*.

Brightly colored worms retract quickly if approached.

Christmas Tree Worm Rock

(Finger, Jewel Stone, Pore, Porous, Worm Rock)

Christmas Tree Worm Rock is not really a rock. Although these worms can be found in live rock, they are usually associated with this coral. The brightly colored worms can make their home in all Porites, but seem especially fond of this type. Since they are dependent on the coral for feeding, if it dies, the worms usually die as well. Because of its difficulty of care, it is not recommended to keep this coral solely for the sake of the Christmas Tree Worms.

Scientific Name: Porites lutea

Cauliflower

Cauliflower is a fairly common SPS coral that can be more light tolerant than many similar species, but it demands high water flow. Many people have had great success with this coral, while others find it very difficult to keep. Cauliflower is one of the largest polyped SPS corals, and some reviewers have suggested that it is not a true SPS coral.

Lighting Needs	6 - 10
Water Flow	H
Aggressiveness	M
Difficulty of Care	8

Prolific raised corallites.

Pink Cauliflower

(Bird's Nest, Branch, Brush, Cluster)

A characteristic unique to Cauliflower is the presence of raised corallites surrounding each branch tip. These certainly account for its descriptive name.

Scientific Name: Pocillopora verrucosa

Cauliflower

This is the most commonly available type of Cauliflower, and is often sold through aquaculture facilities. Such captive bred specimens are often of higher quality since they have adapted to aquarium environments.

Scientific Name: Pocillopora damicornis.

Note comparatively large fluffy polyps.

Frilly Lettuce

(Plate)

Frilly Lettuce is another ridge-like coral whose polyps (like Merulina) are all but invisible. It can be strikingly fluorescent with green highlights on a brown or cream base color, but often does not adapt well to the average aquarium. Some available species prefer a low light and low current environment, while others thrive in the high light and current conditions found on the reef crest.

Scientific Name: Pectinia lactuca

Lighting Needs	6 - 10
Water Flow	M - H
Aggressiveness	L
Difficulty of Care	10

These ridges will extend in a mature colony giving it a "frilly" appearance.

Antler Lettuce

Scientific Name: Pectinia alcicornis

Palm Lettuce

Scientific Name: Pectinia paeonia

Velvet Corals

Velvet corals have possibly the widest and most inconsistent variety of shapes found on the reefs. Velvet corals form massive boulder-like colonies, plate-like slabs, encrusting sheets, and even delicate branches.

There are many variations in color, with common tones of brown, purple and green commonly occurring, although generally in subdued hues. However, in all species the polyps are very uniformly small and fuzzy, giving the coral a velvety appearance.

This is a non-aggressive coral that can be very difficult to keep, but the encrusting and massive varieties are somewhat hardier than the branching types.

Lighting Needs	8 - 10
Water Flow	M - H
Aggressiveness	L
Difficulty of Care	8

Velvet Stone

(Velvet Bush)

Velvet Stone is the name given to any of the massive types of velvet coral. The degree of variation among species is such that almost any shape and color can be possible when purchasing a specimen for the aquarium. The small soft polyps will identify it, and the lack of jewel-like eyes on the skeleton prevents confusion with massive type Jewels.

Scientific Name: Montipora spongodes

Green Velvet Finger

The branching forms of velvet coral, known as Velvet Finger, differ from other branching SPS corals in having rounded ends and a very smooth skeleton. Many times, the branches are somewhat flattened with a slight antler-like appearance.

Scientific Name: Montipora digitata

Purple Velvet Finger

Scientific Name: Montipora digitata

Identification Tip

Look for the smooth, flat, somewhat antler-like branches found on many species of Velvet Finger.

Yellow Velvet Finger

Scientific Name: Montipora digitata

Care Tip

Velvet Finger is a very fragile coral. It is often damaged in shipping and tips are easily broken. However, under favorable conditions, the broken branches can quickly heal and the tips will form new colonies.

SMALL POLYP STONY CORALS

Identification Tip

The cross-hatched ridges help distinguish Ruffled coral from similar species. The valleys and ridges of M. scabricula are random. Those of M. amplicata are short, straight and radiate from the colony center in a fan like pattern. Branching specimens may closely resemble the Horn Corals, but do not have the characteristic hydnophores.

Ruffled Coral

(Ridge, Lettuce)

Ruffled coral is common in nature, occurring in shallow areas of high turbidity. It has extremely small polyps, a ruffled leaf-like skeleton, and a thick mucus coat. It is very difficult to keep in the aquarium because exact light and water quality conditions are required. Ruffled coral is typically brown, tan, pink, and occasionally lime-green with white intermixed. It can appear similar to Frilly Lettuce, but shows a more vertical growth pattern.

Scientific Name: *Merulina scabricula*

Lighting Needs	7 - 10
Water Flow	M - H
Aggressiveness	L
Difficulty of Care	10

Leather Corals

The leather corals are one of many types of soft corals. In nature, these corals would be found in lagoons, and in areas of higher nutrient levels than would be tolerated by stony corals. Reduced turbulence and varying light conditions in nature characterize the ability of these corals to thrive in the aquarium and they can be kept under a broad range of water and lighting conditions. Leather corals do not require feedings, but do benefit from regular iodine additions. All of them can be easily propagated by cutting and grafting.

Leather corals are capable of producing chemical toxins called terpenoids to defend their nook of the reef. Terpenoids can easily kill neighboring corals, so care must be taken to not place them near other species. These substances are most toxic within 8" of the coral, but can theoretically be carried all over the tank.

Leathers go through regenerative stages where they shrink and appear to be dying, and will periodically shed a waxy coat to miraculously renew themselves. This material can drift through the tank and harm other corals that it contacts.

Toadstools

The Toadstools are a huge group of leather corals from the genus Sarcophyton. While commonly available and abundant in nature, they have not been entirely classified. Thus, there is some question as to many actual individual identities. A physical description may be the best way to presently describe some of these corals.

Despite being commonly known as Mushroom Leathers, the overuse of both "mushroom" and "leather" led to the decision to use the name Toadstool instead. Toadstool seems to be more descriptive, and will hopefully eliminate some of the confusion associated with these terms.

All types are extremely hardy corals that tolerate a wide variety of conditions. Toadstools can appear in several colors, but most will become a shade of brown with strong illumination. Some of these corals can grow quite large in the aquarium.

Lighting Needs	2 - 9
Water Flow	L - M
Aggressiveness	M - H
Difficulty of Care	2

Common Toadstool

(Mushroom Leather, Trough, Umbrella)

The Common Toadstool is a frequently available species that will grow very large in the aquarium. This specimen shows the common folded shape that is characteristic of many leather corals.

Scientific Name: Sarcophyton trocheliophorum

Gold Crowned Toadstool

(Golden Crowned Mushroom)

Gold Crowned Toadstool has a heavy trunk with a rounded brown cap. Gold polyps extend outward from the top during the day, giving it a distinct appearance.

Scientific Name: Sarcophyton alcyonidae

Gold polyps just starting to emerge.

Pin Leather Toadstool

The Pin Leather Toadstool is a large species that grows rapidly in the aquarium. The pin-like polyps that protrude upward are quite long in these corals, with the tiny tentacles clearly visible at the tips.

Scientific Name: Sarcophyton sp.

Unusually long "pins".

White Fairy Toadstool

The White Fairy Toadstool is notable for its light tan to pure white coloration and small size.

Scientific Name: Sarcophyton sp.

Green Leather Toadstool
(Milk)

Green Leather Toadstool has a prominent mushroom shape and a translucent, milky-green color. It often turns brown under strong lighting.

Scientific Name: Sarcophyton sp.

LEATHER CORALS

Yellow Toadstool

The Yellow Toadstool is a broad based leather with a distinct yellow color.

Scientific Name: Sarcophyton sp.

Thin stalks will protrude from these pores.

Fancy Yellow Toadstool

Fancy Yellow Toadstool is harder to acclimate to changing water conditions, as would be suggested by its delicate, fluffy appearance.

Scientific Name: Sarcophyton sp.

LEATHER CORALS

Cabbage

(Flower, Lettuce)

Cabbage forms unusual vertical cactus-like colonies that have polyps extending along their top ridges. It is an encrusting leather, and a very hardy species.

Scientific Name: Lobophytum crassum

Note: some reviewers have suggested that this may actually be a Sinularia dura.

Flower Leather

(Fancy Flower)

Flower Leather is a pinkish-brown species with flared ends on its branches or stalks. Small tufted polyps extend outward from the opened flower-like ends. This leather coral is somewhat of a crossover species since it has characteristics of both toadstools and other leather corals.

Scientific Name: Sinularia dura

This specimen is often identified as Lobophytum sp.

Blunt Finger

Blunt Finger exemplifies a common growth pattern in the Lobophytum species. In this case, a broad base and numerous heavy finger-like projections characterize the coral.

Scientific Name: Lobophytum sp.

Note: some reviewers have suggested that this may actually be a Sinularia species.

Devil's Hand

(Chubby Finger, Devil's Claw, Devil's Paw, Scalloped Leather)

Devil's Hand is one of the most easily recognized leather corals because of its abundant availability. This easy to keep species has finger-like projections extruded from a flat palm-like surface, making it resemble an upturned hand. It has a sprinkling of small white tufted polyps that randomly appear on its mustard brown surface when fully expanded. Like most leather corals, the Devil's Hand goes through regular regeneration periods where it fails to expand and sheds a skin. This is not necessarily a sign of poor health.

Scientific Name: Lobophytum pauciflorum

Note the eight petals common to all octocorals.

Devil's Finger

Devil's Finger is very similar to Devil's Hand, but has more finger-like appendages with longer tufted polyps arising from their surfaces.

Scientific Name: Lobophytum sp.

Polyps of Devil's Finger.

Club Finger

Another type of encrusting leather coral, Club Finger, is distinct from the Yellow Encrusting Leather on the next page in having more solid projections arising from the encrusting base. The shorter fingers make it appear less billowy.

Scientific Name: Alcyonium sp.?

Fat Finger

Fat Finger leather has thick colonies of upward growing fingers that give rise to its most descriptive name.

Scientific Name: Lobophytum sp.

Note: some reviewers have suggested that this may actually be a Sinularia species.

Yellow Encrusting

(Bushy Soft, Encrusting Leather, Yellow Bush)

The attractive Yellow Encrusting Leather puts forth short finger-like projections as it encrusts the substrate. Unfortunately, these projections are often cut and offered for sale, so the unique encrusting nature of the coral may not be noticeable. However, this trait will become obvious when the coral attaches to a base and does not form the stalk typical of other leather corals.

Scientific Name: Alcyonium fulvum

Lighting Needs	3 - 8
Water Flow	L - M
Aggressiveness	M
Difficulty of Care	3

Green Finger Leather

Scientific Name: Lobophytum sp.

Soft Corals

Soft corals are a nebulous group of diverse species. Like the leather corals, they lack a calcareous skeleton. Instead, they secrete calcium spicules that aid in supporting their substantial weight and maintaining their shape when inflated. These corals differ from leathers, in that their skin is not as tough, and they appear to be more delicate.

Depending on the species, soft corals can be found from lagoons and silted reef flats to shadowy depths and caves. Some even inhabit the reef crest. As would be apparent from such a variety of habitats, many species are hardy and easy to care for, while others are more difficult to keep successfully.

Single central stalk.

Colt Corals

Colt coral is a popular soft coral that branches upward from a common base. Well-tufted polyps extend from the ends giving it a very fluffy appearance. Despite their availability, there is comparatively little information about Colt corals (including the basis for their name), especially in terms of identification. They can be sliced and attached to other bases as an easy method of propagation. These corals will grow rapidly in almost all conditions, and are **recommended as excellent starter corals**. Most of the Colt corals are brown, pink, or gray.

Scientific Name: Cladiella sp.

Lighting Needs	2 - 8
Water Flow	L - H
Aggressiveness	M
Difficulty of Care	2

Care Tip

Colt corals produce copious amounts of mucus, especially when first introduced into a new tank. This mucus appears to be particularly damaging to SPS corals, so placement "downstream" is highly recommended.

Carnation Corals

The Carnation corals are a large group of brightly colored soft corals that are exclusively ahermatypic (lacking zooxanthellae). Correspondingly, most are found predominantly under ledges and in caves with slow current and dim light. However, many are also found in full light, leading to some confusion about the actual lighting requirements of this coral. Because light is not required, it may be best to avoid possible UV burning of their tissue by placing them in a shaded area of the tank.

Carnations are spectacular and beautiful corals when fully expanded, but are <u>one of the most difficult soft corals to keep in captivity</u>. They require regular feedings of small particulate food, such as baby brine shrimp. For an unknown reason, they are quite unsuccessful when hair algae is present in the aquarium. It is likely that a harmful chemical substance is released by the algae.

Lighting Needs	1 - 4
Water Flow	L - M
Aggressiveness	L
Difficulty of Care	9

Red Carnation

(Strawberry)

Scientific Name: Dendronephthya rubeola

Gold Carnation

(Gold)

Gold Carnation is typical of specimens with a fluffier grouping of polyps. Other Carnations usually have a more stalked appearance.

Scientific Name: Dendronephthya aurea

Note: There are several other beautiful Carnation corals available in the aquarium trade. They have not all been presented because they typically do not fare well in home aquariums. They are one of the most difficult corals to keep in captivity.

Pink Carnation

This species may be tempting to purchase because of its glorious appearance, but most Carnations have a notoriously poor record of survival. **Not recommended.**

Scientific Name: Dendronephthya sp.

Kenya Tree

Although appearing "fluffy", the Kenya Tree has more pronounced branching than the similar Colt. It is also less "soft" to the touch.

Scientific Name: Capnella sp.

Lighting Needs	2 - 6
Water Flow	L - M
Aggressiveness	M
Difficulty of Care	5

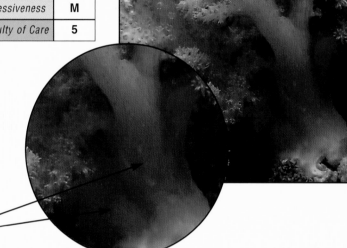

Unlike the Colt corals, the Kenya Tree has multiple main stalks that originate from the base.

Tree Coral

(African Tree, Branch)

Tree Corals are branching species that have a pronounced trunk, branches, and leaf-like polyps. These often brightly colored corals are frequently sold as leather corals, although this is incorrect.

Scientific Name: Lithophyton arboreum

Lighting Needs	2 - 6
Water Flow	M
Aggressiveness	L - M
Difficulty of Care	5

Note the appearance of Tree Coral that is not fully opened.

Neon Green Tree

(Bush, Nephthea, Tree)

Neon Green Tree is a beautiful antler-like soft coral that is part of the large Nephthea genus. Some species do not ship well, and may not acclimate easily to a new tank. Once established, they should be quite hardy and will grow rapidly. This commonly available green species is reported to prefer moderate lighting.

Scientific Name: Nephthea sp.

Lighting Needs	2 - 6
Water Flow	M
Aggressiveness	L - M
Difficulty of Care	6

Note that there is no central stalk.

Medusa

(Sphincter, Christmas Tree)

Medusa coral is unique because of its marked retraction during the night to a condition not unlike some anemones. During the day however, this tan to brown coral unfolds its polyped branches like the snake locks of a Medusa. It sends out tendrils that serve to "root" it in place on the substrate, so it should not be placed on live rock.

Scientific Name: Sphaerella krempfi

Lighting Needs	2 - 5
Water Flow	L - M
Aggressiveness	L
Difficulty of Care	5

The shape of this closed Medusa shows why many people call this Sphincter Coral.

When fully open, this specimen will resemble a dead Christmas tree.

Care Tip

Medusa is ahermatypic, despite its coloration, and must be fed. It also requires a sand or rubble base to thrive.

Finger Corals

Finger corals, while resembling some tree corals, generally have a more antler-like growth pattern. They are all from the genus, *Sinularia*. This is a large and diverse group of corals, especially in terms of color. However, they can be distinguished from the tree corals in that all branches arise from a very prominent and heavy base. Often mistakenly sold as Finger Leather or Colt corals, they differ from Colt in having a less feathery array of polyps.

Finger corals tolerate almost all tank conditions, but become fully open in bright light and will extend flower-like polyps along their length. All species grow quite rapidly, and are easily cut and transposed to form new growths.

These are excellent corals for beginners.

Lighting Needs	2 - 9
Water Flow	M - H
Aggressiveness	M
Difficulty of Care	2

Gold Finger

Scientific Name: Sinularia sp.

Green Finger

Scientific Name: Sinularia sp.

Identification Tip

The Finger corals have a central stalk like Colt corals and polyps similar to tree corals.

Central Stalk

Mauve Finger

Scientific Name: Sinularia sp.

Purple Finger

(Short Cladiella)

This Purple Finger coral has a distinct colorful, berry-like skin with olive green polyps. Despite its atypical form and shape, it is becoming a regular import from the Solomon Islands and Jakarta. Purple finger is often mistakenly imported as Sinularia.

Scientific Name: Cladiella australiensis

Chili

Chili is a branching soft coral that has several color variations. One variety has a pure white skeleton with long, brown, fuzzy polyps that almost obscure the tree-like skeleton. The red form seen in this specimen is probably the origin of its common name.

Scientific Name: Alcyonium sp.

Lighting Needs	3 - 8
Water Flow	L - M
Aggressiveness	M
Difficulty of Care	5

Warty Soft Coral

Warty soft coral resembles Carnation, to which it is closely related. However, it is more solid and opaque looking, and lacks the delicate flower-like polyps. In fact, the polyps on this brightly colored soft coral are grouped in cauliflower-like warts on its extremities, and are randomly scattered over its stalk.

Scientific Name: Scleronepthya sp.

Lighting Needs	2 - 4
Water Flow	L - M
Aggressiveness	L
Difficulty of Care	7

SOFT CORALS

Pulsing Corals, Colonial & Star Polyps

Pulse and waving corals are unique soft corals, highly prized by aquarists because many species actually open and close their polyps rhythmically to filter feed more efficiently. The predominant difference between the pulse (Xenia) and waving (Anthelia) corals is in the origin and shape of their polyps. Waving coral polyps are long and unbranched, all originating from an encrusting mat. Pulse coral polyps arise from a clustered base and are stalked or branched. Both types require regular additions of iodine, and will not accept food.

*T*he colonial and star polyps are a very hardy group of corals consisting of individual polyps that tend to group together. Under good conditions, they can multiply rapidly in the aquarium. The individual polyps are usually clustered together and are found growing on rock or substrate. Some are connected by a rubbery or fibrous mat that quickly encrusts and spreads over tank surfaces. These corals are not dependent on regular feedings, but many will readily take food. Colonial and star polyps can be introduced by happy accident on good quality live rock.

Pulsing and Waving Corals

There is apparently significant confusion and little agreement about the taxonomy of these unique soft corals. References suggest that all species of Anthelia, Xenia, and related Cespitularia can either be of a pulsing or non-pulsing type. Even if a specimen is characterized as non-pulsing, it apparently still has the capacity to do so.

There is similar confusion as to what other physical differences actually exist. Observation and research indicate that xenia polyps tend to be more feathery, although this may not be a definitive characteristic. In general, Anthelia polyps originate from the base, while Xenia originate from a central stalk. Either one may demonstrate pulsing.

Species differ in size, degree of branching, and in color. The blue variations in particular are very appealing. They are also sometimes described by the speed at which the polyps open and close (i.e. fast pulse, slow pulse).

Because of the lack of agreement and surety throughout the hobby regarding these corals, it is recommended that a detailed description of any pulse or waving coral is obtained before purchase. There are many types of pulse and waving coral that have not been covered because of historically inadequate taxonomy and contradictory information.

Pulse corals may not always ship well, and they require a good supply of iodine to thrive and prevent the colony from crashing. However, once established, these corals grow very quickly, encrusting rock rapidly or growing like weeds. They may even require pruning for maximum success and growth rate. Pulse corals prefer moderate to high lighting with a medium to high water flow.

Lighting Needs	5 - 9
Water Flow	M - H
Aggressiveness	L
Difficulty of Care	6

What is Pulsing?

The fascinating pulse corals rhythmically open and close their polyps in a pumping fashion as an aid in gas exchange and feeding. In a way, the pumping action of the polyps mimics the swimming motion of a jellyfish in open water. However, these corals often cease to pulse in the aquarium for unknown reasons. Some sources suggest that terpenes and other chemicals given off by other soft corals may be one possible reason.

Closed

Open

Giant Anthelia

(Giant Xenia, Waving Hand, Giant Pulse, Waving Glove)

Giant Anthelia has large polyps that may be six inches long or more. There is some question as to whether this type is actually a waving coral since it is most often called Giant Xenia. However, it does not have the branching characteristics of a Xenia, and therefore must be assumed to actually be Anthelia. This species usually does not pulse.

Scientific Name: Anthelia glauca

Identification Tip

There has been much confusion about the differences between Anthelia and Xenia. In general, Anthelia polyps originate from the base, while Xenia originate from a central stalk. Either one may demonstrate pulsing.

Pom-Pom

(Pom-Pom Xenia)

The most notably different species of pulse coral occurs mainly as a white tree with puff-like polyped ends clustered on the extremities of thick branches.

Scientific Name: Xenia sp.

Thin Bar

(Pulse Coral, Feather Coral)

This thin-stalked species usually does not pulse.

Scientific Name: Xenia sp.

Silver Tip

(Silver Tip Xenia)

Silver Tip is a striking color variation that is highly prized for its unique appearance.

Scientific Name: Xenia sp.

Note the unique silver tips.

Waving Hand

Waving Hand coral is a long polyped encrusting coral, so named for its resemblance to an arm-like stalk topped by a hand-like polyp. Most species sold do not pulse, although there are specimens that certainly have this characteristic. Some have noted that the ends of Waving Hand coral are less feathery and have shorter tips, although this is not a universally recognized attribute. These corals seem slightly hardier in the aquarium, and are less prone to the colony crashes of pulse corals.

Scientific Name: Anthelia sp.

Tree Xenia

Scientific Name: Xenia elongata

Umbrella Xenia

(Glove Xenia)

Scientific Name: Xenia umbellata

Identification Tip

Umbrella's polyps begin projecting horizontally in a hemispherical array from the main stalk.

Button Polyps

Button polyps are a very common and prolific group of colonial polyps, closely related to anemones. They provide somewhat of a bridge between the species. Stalked with a flat mushroom-like disc, fine tentacles radiate from the outer edge of the disc. The polyps are colonial in nature, and may be connected to each other, especially by budding. They are not, however, connected by a common base.

Button polyps adapt well to almost all light regimes, although bright light tends to make their colors more vibrant. They are extremely hardy in the aquarium, and they will reproduce easily. Although it is not required, button polyps can be fed small bits of food. They require iodine for proper health.

These are excellent corals for beginners.

Lighting Needs	2 - 8
Water Flow	M
Aggressiveness	L
Difficulty of Care	1

Green Button Polyps

Scientific Name: Zooanthus pulchellus

Brown Button Polyps

Scientific Name: Zooanthus sociatus

Polyps are connected, but not matted or encrusting.

Caution!

Despite their non-aggressive nature, some members of Zooanthus secrete palytoxins in their mucus. These potentially deadly substances are only dangerous if mucus contacts a cut or break in the skin.

Gold Sea Mat

Scientific Name: Palythoa sp.

Sea Mats

Sea mats may be almost indistinguishable from button polyps, and are often sold as such. However, the sea mat polyps are part of a fibrous encrusting mat, and individuals cannot be separated from their neighbors without cutting through the mat that binds them. While they adapt to most conditions, strong light is essential for maintaining the often bright colors of the polyps.

These are excellent corals for beginners.

Lighting Needs	3 - 9
Water Flow	M
Aggressiveness	L
Difficulty of Care	2

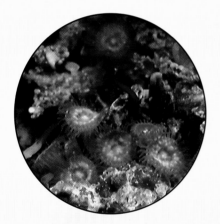

Blue Sea Mat

Scientific Name: Palythoa sp.

Fibrous encrusting "mat".

Red Sea Mat

Scientific Name: Palythoa sp.

Orange Sea Mat

Scientific Name: Palythoa sp.

Grand Polyp

The Grand Polyp, though classified as belonging to the genus of sea mats, does not really fit in well with the rest of the group. It is more like a large button polyp in both appearance and growth.

Scientific Name: Palythoa grandis

Clove Polyps

Clove Polyps, resemble some waving corals (Anthellia), but they have thicker stalks, a knobby mat, and retract completely at night. They may also have contrasting centers.

Scientific Name: Clavularia sp.

Moon Polyp

The Moon Polyp is unique for its upward turning cup and delicate appearance.

Scientific Name: Palythoa sp.

Yellow Polyps

Classically hydroid in shape, Yellow Polyps are a popular and common addition to reef tanks. Despite being colonial, each polyp is truly individual. Their shape is somewhat uncommon, with fine long tentacles radiating from a thinner fluted body.

Through an unknown mechanism (probably a local chemical messenger), the polyps either open or close in unison when favorable or unfavorable stimuli are present, as if they were a single connected group.

Yellow polyps are very hardy, light tolerant, and reproduce easily in the aquarium. They also enjoy a light feeding from time to time, although this is not necessary.

Scientific Name: Parazoanthus gracilis

Star Polyps

Star polyps are connected together by a bumpy, purple, rubbery mat from which long grassy polyps emerge. Cream, white, tan, and green are common colors, although star polyps can be found in other shades. In fact, this mat is so hardy that it can easily grow over rocks and even glass. The mat can be cut easily and tied on a rock, and it will soon attach to and begin covering its new base. These are very durable and beautiful polyps that truly look like a field of colorful wheat blowing in the breeze. Highly recommended.

Lighting Needs	2 - 9
Water Flow	M
Aggressiveness	L
Difficulty of Care	1

Daisy Polyps

Daisy Polyps have a pronounced flower-like appearance with shorter terminating polyp ends and yellow centers.

Scientific Name: Clavularia sp.

Brown Star Polyps

Scientific Name: Clavularia sp.

Green Star Polyps

A very interesting tank in Atlanta has a lawn of Green Star Polyps across the bottom aquarium glass that is "mowed" by trimming the mat as it begins to creep up the glass sides.

Scientific Name: Clavularia viridis

Gold Star Polyps

Scientific Name: Clavularia sp.

Flowering Star Polyps

Scientific Name: Clavularia sp.

Identification Tip

Snake Polyp is easily distinguished by the prominent bumps on the stalks. In fact, the species name means "little knot".

Snake Polyps

Snake Polyps are very odd looking creatures that are just now starting to show up with some frequency in the hobby. In the wild, they are often found as unremarkable solitary animals attached to something just below the surface of the sand. However, colonial groups such as this specimen can be really spectacular. They appear to be easy to care for, tolerating a wide variety of lighting and water flow conditions.

Scientific Name: Isaurus tuberculatus?

Stick Polyps

Stick Polyps are parasites that form on the tissue of certain species of sponge. The sponge eventually dies and leaves the appearance of a stick covered with polyps. The entire colony is collected while still adhering to its old host.

Interestingly, there are several different species of polyps that parasitize many different sponges and other aquatic life. Stick polyps are not commonly available.

Scientific Name: Parazoanthus swiftii

These black tips are an unusual color morph.

The Gorgonians

The gorgonians are an immensely large group of prolific species called Octocorals, having eight petaled tentacles. They dominate many areas of the reef where stony corals do not occur as frequently, many of these corals are often unavailable to hobbyists, while others are regularly offered. There is very little taxonomic distinction available to the aquarist to help in an often obscure identification process. Almost every genus has many members that differ in color, size, naturally occurring depth, and even shape. This fact makes it difficult to provide proper lighting and current data, since the different species may or may not be tolerant of a broad range of conditions outside their specific point of collection. Gorgonians can become quite tall and reach from the bottom to the top of an aquarium. Thus, the whole specimen will be exposed to potentially great variances in lighting intensity within the tank.

Gorgonians are filter feeders, but many readily accept small pieces of food blown across their polyps. Their chance of survival is greater if they are still attached by their base (holdfast) to a clutch of rock. Once established, they are quite successful in a properly managed aquarium. Generally, gorgonians with thick fingers are hardier and more successful than ones with thin fingers. Brown or tan polyps are indicative of easier-to-keep photosynthetic gorgonians. Because they are not true stony corals, gorgonians may be legally sold when collected from Caribbean waters.

For the most part, gorgonians can be the hardest to keep of the soft corals. Many require water conditions similar to the stony corals, and in some cases are even more demanding. Sea fans, for example, rarely survive for long in the aquarium.

Silver Gorgonian

(Quill)

This unusual and attractive gorgonian is not commonly available. However, aquaculture techniques now being developed, will provide hardy, aquarium-ready specimens in the very near future

Scientific Name: Muricea laxa

Lighting Needs	3 - 9
Water Flow	M - H
Aggressiveness	L
Difficulty of Care	7

Encrusting Gorgonians

Encrusting gorgonians grow from a creeping mat like Corky Fingers, but do not send forth any pronounced finger-like projections. Growing over rocks and substrate, the mat is fairly smooth, and the fine fuzzy polyps rise from pores in the mat. Polyps arising from the pores distinguishes encrusting gorgonian from the sea mats and star polyps. They must be sold attached to a piece of substrate.

Encrusting Boulder

Scientific Name: Briareum sp.

Encrusting Carpet

Scientific Name: Erythropodium sp.

Corky Finger

Corky Fingers is an encrusting gorgonian found in both the Atlantic and Pacific oceans. Some types will put forth finger-like projections from the mat, but most "fingers" result from the rapid encrustation of other surfaces that include other living gorgonians and corals. The Corky Fingers to the left has begun covering some Sea Blades. This gorgonian has a purple mat with raised calyces and usually olive-green polyps.

Scientific Name: Briareum asbestinum

Lighting Needs	4 - 9
Water Flow	M - H
Aggressiveness	L
Difficulty of Care	5

The "rabbit ears" projecting from this specimen are actually a Sea Blade that has been almost completely encrusted.

Orange Finger

(Colorful Sea Rod, Orange Tree)

Orange Finger is a commonly available species that has sparse and stick-like orange or yellow branches dotted with red nodules from which snow white tufted polyps emerge. These gorgonians are non-photosynthetic and require feeding.

Scientific Name: Diodogorgia nodulifera

Lighting Needs	2 - 6
Water Flow	M - H
Aggressiveness	L
Difficulty of Care	7

Red Finger

(Colorful Sea Rod, Red Tree)

Another equally common gorgonian is the Red Finger. It has red branches, dark red nodules, and white polyps.

Scientific Name: Diodogorgia nodulifera

Purple Sea Blade

(Whips)

Sea Blades are another fairly large and diverse group of gorgonians in terms of size, shape and color. These are almost exclusively shallow to mid-depth gorgonians. They are most easily distinguished by having flatter branches with polyps arising from the blade like edges. Most branch in a single plane and the white polyps indicate a non-photosynthetic coral that requires feeding.

Scientific Name: Pterogorgia guadalupensis

Lighting Needs	6 - 8
Water Flow	M - H
Aggressiveness	L
Difficulty of Care	7

Gold Sea Blade

(Whips)

Scientific Name: Pterogorgia anceps

Note flat blade branch.

This specimen is branching in a single plane, although this is not always a distinguishing characteristic.

Purple Sea Plume

(Purple Americana, Purple Frilly)

The Purple Sea Plume is most easily recognized by having branches with central spines from which nearly equal length quills branch off, giving it the appearance of a plume. The polyps extend from the thin extensions branching off the central spine, and are usually the same color as the gorgonian itself.

Scientific Name: *Pseudopterogorgia bipinnata*

Lighting Needs	5 - 10
Water Flow	M - H
Aggressiveness	L
Difficulty of Care	6

Yellow Sea Plume

(Yellow Frilly, Slimy Sea Plumes)

The Yellow Sea Plume is similar to the Purple Sea Plume. Like its purple variation, the plumes generally branch in a single plane, making this type of gorgonian easier to recognize.

Scientific Name: *Pseudopterogorgia bipinnata*

Candelabra

(Swollen Knob, Knobby Rod, Warty Rod)

Candelabras are gorgonians distinguished by numerous thick and bent branches which retain a very bumpy surface when the polyps are retracted. Although a typically shallow water species, the colors and requirements for care vary dramatically, depending on the species and location of collection.

Scientific Name: Eunicea mammosa

Lighting Needs	5 - 10
Water Flow	M - H
Aggressiveness	L
Difficulty of Care	4

Thick branches remain flexible.

Red Sea Spray

Sea Sprays have branches that are very thin, sparse, and twig-like, and they retain a bumpy appearance when the polyps are retracted. Colors common to this type are shades of red and orange.

Scientific Name: Leptogorgia sp.

Lighting Needs	3 - 9
Water Flow	M - H
Aggressiveness	L
Difficulty of Care	8

Note bumpy appearance of branches.

Porous Sea Rod

The Porous Sea Rod has distinctive, round, pore-like, polyp apertures. By contrast, the closely related Slit-Pore Sea Rod (Plexaurella sp.) has polyp apertures that resemble small cuts covering the branches.

Scientific Name: Pseudoplexaura sp.

Lighting Needs	4 - 10
Water Flow	M - H
Aggressiveness	L
Difficulty of Care	4

Polyp apertures of the Slit-Pore Sea Rod resemble small cuts.

Knobby Sea Rod

(Brown Sea Rod)

This gorgonian has highly branched, spindly rods with a knobbed surface. Colors vary, but purple and brown are predominant.

Scientific Name: Eunicea sp.

Care Note

Knobby Sea Rod has a notoriously poor survival rate in reef aquariums. Many dealers are no longer stocking this species.

Mushroom Anemones
& Other Corallimorphs

Discosoma and Actinodiscus are the genera that comprise the mushroom anemones, whose morphology lies somewhere between corals and anemones. They are structurally similar to anemones, but are not such aggressive feeders.

Variations within the mushroom anemones are almost limitless. They appear in hundreds of vivid hues. There are tiny mushrooms only an inch in diameter, and giant mushrooms almost a foot across. There are metallic mushrooms, striped mushrooms, fuzzy mushrooms, knobby mushrooms, hairy mushrooms, etc.

Species determination is almost impossible, since phenotypically similar specimens from different oceans may be of a completely different genus.

All mushroom anemones should be attached to a rock or base when purchased. They can expand dramatically when placed in a low current location in the tank. Iodine is essential for proper coloration, and for maximum expansion and reproduction. These are very hardy corals and can be kept under virtually all light conditions, although direct metal halide light and strong current will prevent full expansion.

The Mushrooms:
Contact Problems

Although the mushroom anemones have traditionally been considered to be benign and harmless, recent evidence suggests that they actually can injure corals that they directly contact. Even the notoriously aggressive Galaxea is not immune. Oddly enough, these are non-aggressive, non-stinging corals with no known chemical release. Therefore, the mechanism for this "passive-aggressiveness" is not known.

Lighting Needs	**2 - 6**
Water Flow	**L**
Aggressiveness	**L**
Difficulty of Care	**2**

COLOR VARIATIONS

There are many colors of mushrooms, and a few typical color variations are shown here. The colors are found in combination with other physical variations in pattern, size, and surface texture, and are dependent on the actual specimen. The most common colors are blue, red, green, and purple. The colors may also change somewhat when introduced to new conditions.

Some of the patterns found on mushrooms can be quite striking. Stripes, speckles, rings, and patches are all commonly occurring variations.

Plain

Speckled or Mottled

Striped

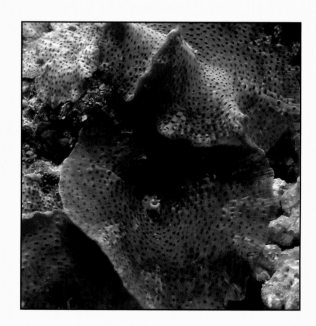

Spotted

MUSHROOM ANEMONES

TEXTURE VARIATIONS

The texture of mushroom anemones is quite diverse. Some have long protuberances that look like hair. Others have bumps, warts, fuzz, ridges, folds, or are smooth surfaced. Textures may change from day to day, to some extent becoming more or less pronounced.

Smooth

Hairy

Frilly

Fuzzy

MUSHROOM ANEMONES

Bubble Mushroom

Some mushroom anemones do not grow flat against the surface to which they are attached. Many have raised stalks, a round bubble-like cap, or folds that elevate their surface. The Caribbean Bubble Mushrooms prefer low light to retain their beautiful colors. They can be up to 4" in diameter.

Scientific Name: *Discosoma sanctithomas*

Care Tip

When a Bubble Mushroom is stressed, injured, or otherwise unhappy, it will commonly expel its innards. Low light and good water flow is recommended to help it recover.

Umbrella Mushroom

(Atlantic Corallimorph)

This attractive Caribbean species comes in several different colors and can be up to 4" in diameter. It reportedly reproduces by division at the "foot".

Scientific Name: *Discosoma neglecta*

Elephant Ear and Giant mushrooms are so named for their size. As many color and texture variations exist among these giants as in any other type of mushroom anemone. Rhodactis can eat food, including fish, by producing a bubble trap on its surface. It may swell out substantially after feeding. Some clownfish will accept Giant mushrooms of the Rhodactis genus as surrogates for their host anemones.

Elephant's Ear

Scientific Name: Rhodactis sp.

Giant Cup in fully open state.

Giant Cup

(Elephant Ear)

Scientific Name: Amplexidiscus sp.

Giant Brown

Scientific Name: Rhodactis sp.

Giant Mushroom

Scientific Name: Rhodactis sp.

MUSHROOM ANEMONES

Ricordea

Ricordea is found only in Florida and Caribbean waters. It is a small to medium size mushroom, characterized by unique contrasting round raised dots across its surface. The colors of Ricordea can vary from orange to blue, green, brown, and even purple, but they can lose their bright, fluorescent colors under intense lighting. Ricordea is still legally available from Florida waters, but the rock it attaches to is not. Therefore, collectors are now shipping individual polyps instead of "Ricordea Rock".

Scientific Name: Ricordea florida

This species of Actinodiscus from the Indo-Pacific and African Coasts is being imported as Ricordea. Despite an obviously close resemblance, this species is not Ricordea, but is a variation of the fuzzy texture.

Florida Mushroom

(Forked Tentacle)

Scientific Name: Discosoma carlgreni

Flower Anemone

The Flower Anemone is more closely related to an anemone than a mushroom and it may be the true link between the species. An active feeder, this colorful mushroom remains stationary, but is taxonomically classified as an anemone. Anemones are related to corals because they are invertebrates that contain zooxanthellae in their tissues. Many beautiful species exist, and identification of these creatures as well as many other common reef invertebrates will be included in the next book in our "Practical Guide" series.

... A genetic link between the corals and the true anemones

INDEX

INDEX BY COMMON NAME

INDEX BY COMMON NAME

INDEX BY SCIENTIFIC NAME

INDEX BY SCIENTIFIC NAME

Suggested Reading:

Reef Coral Identification, by Paul Humann

Marine Invertebrates, vol. 1, by Peter Wilkens

Marine Invertebrates, vol. 2, by Peter Wilkens and Johannes Birkholz

Indo-Pacific Coral Reef Field Guide, by Dr. Gerald R. Allen and Roger Steene

The Reef Aquarium, by J. Charles Delbeek and Julian Sprung

Tropical Pacific Invertebrates, by Patrick L. Colin and Charles Arneson

Corals of Australia and the Indo-Pacific, by J.E.N. Veron

A Field Guide to Coral Reefs, by Eugene H. Kaplan

The Greenpeace Book of Coral Reefs, by Sue Wells and Nick Hanna

Coral Reefs, a Global View by diver Les Holiday, by Les Holiday

A Natural History of the Coral Reef, by Charles R.C. Shepard

Marine Atlas, by Helmut Debelius and Hans A. Braensch

Manual of Marine Invertebrates, by Tetra Press

Dynamic Aquaria: Building Living Ecosystems, by W. H. Adey and K. Loveland

Marine Invertebrates and Plants of the Living Reef, by Dr. Patrick L. Collin

Encyclopedia of Marine Invertebrates, edited by Jerry G. Walls

Reefkeeper's Arm "Coral"

(Compulsive Tank Organizer)

This *"coral"* is never found in the wild, but is an extremely common sight in home reef aquariums. It comes in several different colors and unlimited variations in hue and shading. It is ahermatypic and must be fed constantly, as would be suggested by the long *"finger-like"* polyps. Although a few specimens prefer vegetable diets, most prefer regular feedings of Margaritas, fresh shrimp and Key Lime Pie (Caribbean).

This *"coral"* can be the most difficult of all to care for, as it is highly impulsive and unpredictable (especially the male of the species). It is always very expensive to maintain, a fact that must be considered carefully before committing to many years of care. One thing is for certain though, the Reefkeeper's Arm needs lots of TLC (tender loving care), especially when the sump overflows and floods the living room downstairs.

Scientific Name: Homo sapiens (subspecies: reefaquariensis)

NOTE: Some reviewers have suggested that this actually may not be a "coral" at all, but simply the arm of reefkeepers everywhere who have spent WAY too much time re-arranging their live rock. We will leave that up to the taxonomists to decide.

Lighting Needs	M - Colors tend to change drastically under varying lighting conditions.
Water Flow	H - Reefkeepers by nature need constant water flow.
Aggressiveness	L - Except when threatened by invading Mantis Shrimp.
Difficulty of Care	H - Needs lots of "TLC" to thrive.

Thanks, we hope you have enjoyed this book. For more information about upcoming projects, be sure to check out our web site at:

http://members.aol.com/octocoral/corals.htm

Ed & Eric :-)